POEMS OF THE ENGLISH COUNTRYSIDE

POEMS OF THE ENGLISH COUNTRYSIDE

DOREEN BEER

MERLIN BOOKS LTD.,
Braunton, England.

To the giver of all gifts — for eyes to see;
To Hilda my mother — for encouragement;
Susan and Sally my daughters — for listening;
my husband for love and support,
and my grandchildren that it may instil in them
a love of nature and ongoing inspiration.

First published in Great Britain, 1996

British Library Cataloguing in Publication Data
A catalogue record for this book is available from the British Library

ISBN 0 86303 739-9

Printed in England by Orchard & Ind Ltd., Gloucester

ENGLAND IS POETRY

England — gentle undulating hills,
Wild heather covered moorlands,
Serene, shimmering lakes
And surging, silvery seas.
England — celebrated cathedral cities,
Peaceful pastoral pathways,
Flower filled meadows,
Fertile, fruitful orchards.
England — gardens gloriously arrayed
Pansies — poppies — roses:
And rugged rambling rockeries,
Of campions and sea pinks
Overhanging the ocean.
England — homely harbours,
Pristine, painted boats
And wheeling white gulls;
Cornfields of gold,
Pastures of green,
Sheep and cows contentedly grazing,
Children playing by village streams
And quaint old bridges
Of rough hewn stone.
England is all this — and more
So much more —
England is poetry
Written indelibly on the hearts
Of all who love her.

THE TRANQUIL HEART

If you would have a tranquil heart
And a contented mind
Then you must seek out nature's peace,
It is not hard to find;
In tree lined park or country lane,
Beside a quiet pool
On verdant hill, in forest glade
It waits with calm and cool.

And when you've found the tranquil heart
Then you will somehow know
It surely was the hand of God,
Which touched and made it so.
For every form of leaf and flower,
Tree, watercourse and stone
God made with pleasure, love and care
To lead man to his throne.

ONLY A DAISY

It was not an exotic orchid
Which lifted my spirit so high,
Nor yet an elegant garden rose
Which brought tears of joy to the eye.

It was only a tiny daisy,
Blushed pink and exquisitely sweet,
Which a small child gently delivered
From being trodden under my feet.

So tenderly rescued from crushing,
And presented with more of its kind,
With love in the eyes of the giver
And joy at the wealth of her find.

BEAUTY

Beauty is a feast to the eyes,
A wonder to the mind,
A joy to the heart,
An inspiration to the soul
And infinitely more.
Beauty is mystical,
For who can explain it?
A thing of beauty may be touched;
Yet beauty is intangible.
Beauty is a tiny flower
And a mighty mountain.
Beauty illuminates a second
And beauty is eternal,
For beauty never ceases,
It is ever with us —
Somehow, somewhere;
Beauty draws us to the seas,
To the rivers and moors,
To woodlands and hills
And to all wonders of creation.
Beauty speaks of God,
Brings us close to God
And is given by God;
Beauty can be wrapped in thought
And presented in words —
Beauty is life's gift.

MY HILL

My hill is greened by sprouting wheat
And nature urges on my feet
To walk upon that lovely brow
To feel and know that God is now.

My hill is golden as the morn
That smiles upon the ripened corn
And when I lift my eyes that way
My thoughts are gilded by His ray.

My hill is brown — the furrow's ploughed
The seed is sown with life endowed
And all His mystery lies beneath
My hill, and heals my unbelief.

My hill is white, aloof and still;
But never lovelier — my hill,
Majestic in its mantle bright
It wings my heart to realms of light.

My hill is blue and shadowed black
My hill is everything I lack,
Solid, steadfast, fruitful, wise,
Could I be so to seeking eyes?

My hill is framed the seasons through
Within my window clear to view,
Every morning when I rise
How can I fail to lift my eyes.

ONE SNOWDROP SMALL

Born of the snow,
Bathed in the dew
Dressed by the frost,
Her fairness grew.
Kissed by the breeze,
Blessed by the rain
Softly she spoke
Of spring again.
Cold was the soil,
Dark was her bed,
Strong was the faith
Which upward led;
No warmth she knew,
Except inside
Her tiny heart,
From which spread wide
The warmth and start
Of every spring,
Its new sprung hope
Its wondering.
One snowdrop small
And sweet as love,
One fragile link
With heaven above.

SOMEONE HAD WATCHED

From the thickening hedgetop rose,
A mallard duck on whirring wing,
Which prompted us to seek and find
Her nest near by — for it was spring.

A cosy, lovely, work of art
It was, for such as she, who owned
Nothing to aid her in this work,
Seven eggs lay beautifully enthroned.

Three weeks passed by and yet again,
We trod the self same path which led
To where the nest lay empty, cold,
We thought — 'are they alive or dead?'

And then our feet turned to the brook
Which meandered by so merrily,
On whirring wing she rose — what fright!
What thrill! so unexpectedly.

There were her precious fluffy brood
Clustered happily in the grass,
Just where we chanced to wander by,
Who led our feet this way to pass?

Homeward we trod with happy hearts,
For having witnessed such a sight.
In this wild creature's world, we knew
Someone had watched — they were all right.

PRECIOUS PEARLS

Pearls of poetry are sometimes sent
When they are least expected,
To be patiently re-strung,
Polished and perfected.
Cultured, lustrous, strings of rhyme
For human hearts to treasure,
Precious pearls of poetry
Thread through a lifetime's pleasure.

JOY FOR EVERYONE

Joy is the overspill of gladness
It is a perfect dawn fresh rose,
Joy intermingles with all sadness;
Joy is poetry and prose.
Joy is the music of the earth,
Songbirds and singing streams,
Joy is the summer's birth,
Living life — fulfilling dreams.
Joy is contentment of the heart,
A baby's smiling eyes,
Appreciation of an art;
Joy is that gift of sweet surprise.
Joy is love — a priceless treasure,
Yet joy is free and joy is there,
In little things, in ample measure,
Joy for everyone to share.

WHEN I LOOK UPON A TREE

I never cease to wonder
When I look upon a tree,
Vivid in its autumn dress,
Or in sweet simplicity
Wearing the buds of springtime,
Or with blossom newly crowned,
Tiptoeing to touch the sky,
Or weeping to the ground.

I never cease to wonder
When I look upon a tree,
Radiant as the moonlight
Silvers all the tracery,
Outlining every twiglet,
Each curving bough and branch,
My eyes are blessed with beauty
At every upward glance.

TO CELANDINES

O tiny flowers of minted gold,
Coined deep inside the earth's dark mine,
Braving the ice of winter's edge,
Reflectors of the first sunshine.

I love to see you by the verge,
Or starring countless grassy banks,
A power you have to raise my mind
Evoking to our Maker thanks.

Thanks that I have the eyes to see
Your beauty — and a heart to know,
That in nature's smallest flowerets
His love and mine together flow.

ACORNS

Acorns are on the oaks again
And ears are on the corn,
Assurance of homes and sustenance
For songsters yet unborn;
Sloes are on the blackthorn,
Ripe hips flame the briar;
In schemes to beautify the land
All nature does conspire.

Berries are on the rowan trees
Hazels mature in woods,
Squirrels and field mice gather
Their store of winter foods.
There's a promise around each corner,
Symbols of hope and cheer.
Acorns are on the oak again
As Autumn blesses the year.

The silver birches are gilded
With gold — and sumachs show
The blazing colours of embers
Reflecting the bonfire's glow:
There's a mistiness in the morning
And a radiance on the day,
Acorns are on the oaks again
A future forest in sway.

VALE OF THE EXE

How green is my valley
Down here in the west,
For this blessed place
Holds all I love best,
To leave this fair scene
It would my heart vex;
This beautiful, verdant,
Vale of the Exe.

How green is the woodland
Of oak, ash and beech
In shades intermingled
Which compliment each;
How diverse the bird life,
How varied their songs.
In this lovely Exe valley
Where my heart belongs.

How green are the meadows
Through which the Exe flows
And glorious the flora
That blossoms and blows;
How rich are the gardens
With produce and fruit,
How fertile this haven
Where the Exe carves its route.

THE SPIRIT OF THE RIVER

There is never an end to a river,
Even when it reaches the seas,
For the eddies and swirls of its waters
Retain immortal land memories;
There's the green of the trees in its flowing
And the sweet wholesome breath of the wheat,
The fragrance of meadowland flowers
And a dark undercurrent of peat;
It carries the glitter of sunlight,
The reflection of summer blue sky,
Murmuring voices of countryside,
Are gathered from far off and nigh,
Colour and perfume, movement and sound
Are absorbed in slow or swift motion:
There is never an end to a river
For its spirit lives on in the ocean.

ENGLAND'S JOYS

A garden full of glorious flowers
Is one of England's joys
'Though but common cottage blooms
Their pleasure never cloys.

England's colours predominate
In roses red and white,
Madonna lilies, peonies,
Blue cornflowers, pansies bright.

Walk country lane or village street,
You will find them in employ,
The gardeners of England
Who light our eyes with joy.

BLUEBELLS

As April makes her yearly bow
And May comes dancing through,
A mist appears in copse and dell,
A mist of heaven's own blue.

And bells ring out, 'though human ears
Catch not their ding-a-ling,
For fairy folk in woodland glade
Alone hear bluebells ring.

Tossed by the breeze each dainty bell
Wafts sweetness on the air;
And for the wee fay's parties
Make magic music rare.

And every strange and wondrous thought
That filters through my brain,
Is fanned into reality
As I walk the bluebell lane.

TO A BLACKBIRD

Blackbird,
You have nothing to relieve
Your uniformity of garb,
Except the crocus yellow
Of that brilliant barb,
Which stabs repeatedly
At the dampened lawn:
To pull there from
A wriggling worm at dawn.

Blackbird,
No dazzling hues are thine
Your plumage sombre black
And dull dun brown your mate;
Yet there is no lack
Of glory in your stance;
Those topaz circled eyes
Hold all the brightness
Of the first sun rise.

THE APPLE HARVEST

The brown breath of Autumn
Hangs on the warm air,
Lingering lazily
In branches now bare,
Spent apples lie rotting
Rich juices outpour,
Parental tree rootlets
Reabsorb and re-store.

With hawthorns and rosehips
The orchard is framed,
Picked apples in boxes
Are sunshine inflamed;
Ripe hazels are spilling
Plop! Plop! in the stream
As we wend our way home
To fruit pie and cream.

A SUMMER EVENING GATHERING

The rain fresh herbage breathed its breath
Upon the evening air,
Flowers, leaves and tendrils lent
Each their own sweet share.

Breezes merged and intermingled,
Yarrow, woodsage and fern,
One fragrance scarcely singled
For senses to discern.

Elderflower and wild clover,
Honeysuckle, rose entwined,
Permeated one another,
Suffused, confused the mind.

And 'though perplexed by such a mix
Of scents from far and near;
Yet indelibly the senses fix
The perfume of the year.

The perfume of the summer time
Evocative as a tune,
I would capture in its prime
And I would name it 'June'.

THE BLISS OF SOLITUDE

I walked alone upon the hills
(Envisaging those 'Daffodils')
And while my head was in the cloud,
My mind a thoughtful furrow ploughed,
As in the vale below I spied
A host of flowers drifting wide,
Beside the stream, beneath the trees,
In procession, poised to please;
(Not Daffodils, they'd bloomed and gone),
Bluebells en masse I gazed upon,
Continuous as a rippling ocean.
Moving, merging — great emotion
Rose within me at this scene,
I was, where Wordsworth once had been;
Although these hills were not the same,
Although myself knew not his fame,
That exultation deep inside
Would like his, with me abide:
Oft now I sit indoors and see
This vision blue — although each tree
Has shed sere leaves and winds blow cold
The picture's framed in memory's hold
'To flash upon the inward eye'
And lift the weary spirit high.

TALKING TIME IS OVER

What are we doing to our world?
Destroying plants and trees,
Endangering wild animals,
And acting as we please.

We were sent as guardians,
The continuance to ensure
Of this our own great planet,
Why then make it poor?

Why are we polluting rivers,
Lovely lakes and seas?
Why are men so careless?
When life depends on these.

From the smallest creature living,
To the largest on the earth,
Another life is dependant,
It's chain of mighty girth.

And when a link is broken
And many links are stressed,
Their weakness will be passed in time
To many of the rest.

Talking time is over,
Action must begin,
Or mankind's own extinction
Will be mankinds own sin.

THE MEADOWLANDS OF ENGLAND

Where are the rolling meadowlands
Of my childhood's delight?
With feathery flowering grasses
All silver mauve and white,
Filled with the breath of clover
And the hum of many bees,
Quenched by unpolluted brooks
And sheltered by elm trees.

Where have they gone, these meadowlands?
Which flowed like moving seas,
Children, butterflies and birds
Knew paradise in these;
Cranesbill and ragged robin,
Lady's smock and meadowsweet
Lent perfume to the summer air
And pollened small bare feet.

Those meadowlands are memories,
Those flowers fewer by far,
Butterflies endangered,
As we 'progress' in grit and tar.
More carparks, roads and bridges,
Carve England's lovely face;
But a word is 'conservation',
As we yearly lose more space.

ALCHEMILLA

Rain had fallen through the night,
Dawn lit the day with pearled light,
Out in the garden fresh — the sun
Sparked and glinted — spiders spun
Tiny wheels, 'twixt flower and leaf
And beauty was beyond belief.

As I breathed a thankful sigh,
An alchemilla caught my eye,
This modest 'lady's mantle' green
Wore diamonds of most brilliant sheen;
Queen of the morning crowned was she
And gloried her simplicity.

A POET'S RESPONSE

I love to read the wisdom
Within the words of those
Whose eyes have perceived nature,
In all its ebbs and flows,
Beheld and grasped with subtle power
Ingenious creation,
Unveiled in leaf, snowflake or flower,
Compelling observation.

I love to probe and comprehend
What moved those bards to write,
Of simple things, in special ways,
My own heart to delight;
Opening up response in me,
To seek the gems they sought;
Hence in finding and exulting,
Through poetry I am taught.

'TRANQUILLITY'

T ouch a flower
R ecall a song,
A ssuage a sorrow
N egate a wrong
Q uest true peace
U nite the divided,
I nstil a calm
L ight the misguided,
L ift the weary
I nspire humility
T rust in God
Y ours — 'Tranquillity'.

SERENITY

S oothing sounds of singing stream,
E merald light of vernal wood,
R oseate warmth of sunset's gleam
E ase of mind at wrong withstood:
N ature keeps to peace — the key,
I nherent blessings in her hold,
T rust her and know serenity;
Y ield heart and mind, let calm enfold.

PEACE

P aint a picture from a memory,
E levate the mind with gladness,
A ctivate a dormant talent,
C onsole a friend in time of sadness
E arn someone's trust — faith increase
your recompense is peace.

THE UNSEEN VIOLET

In a quiet secluded nook
Within a forest glade,
There's a newly opened violet
Peeping through dense shade.

A natural observance?
For beauty seeking eyes —
I was not the gem's surveyor,
I did not this treasure prize.

In fact no human eyes will light,
Today, next week or ever,
Upon this springtime flower,
For providence was clever.

Upon a lonesome spot, the seed
Was blown and sown by chance,
Where human walkers seldom tread,
Where children's feet ne'er dance.

And so unbruised and perfect,
The violet nods a while,
With only birds and beasts to greet
Its sweet and modest smile.

DEVONSHIRE

D awn opens up her door to light
E ternal hills in colours bright,
V eins of gold through purple thread,
O pal pools glint from sphagnum bed.
N orth to South and East to West,
S unlight and shadows move and rest:
H eathery heights and verdant coombes,
I nterfuse their wild perfumes;
R ed deer roam and buzzards glide.
E xe winds to Exeter — Devon's pride.

THORVERTON

Take a journey here and view
Happy rural life portrayed,
Observe herein traditions
Reflect, — watch cricket played;
Various village pastimes,
Enable residents to be
Relaxed, released, refreshed,
Take a vacation here and see.
Oh how I love the place of my birth,
Nucleus of all things of worth.

A WINTER'S SCENE

Imagine now a winter's scene,
When naught is white, yet naught is green;
But etched in colours indistinct,
Greyish pencilled, bluish inked,
Birds and branch one tinge they seem,
Ponds and puddles lose their gleam
A sun abandoned scene for certain,
All sky is draped in sombre curtain.
barren branches, tangled rise
In silhouettes against the skies,
Wind plants iced kisses on the brow,
Then seeks tall pines to sigh and sough.
Imagine this scene and visualize —
See winter in poetic guise.

THE LONESOME ROSE

On Christmas day I spied a rose
Blooming gloriously,
Its petals rivalled robin's breast
And rubied holly tree;
Alone of all its kind, it stood
Supreme above the snow,
Lending that cold winter's day
A touch of summer's glow.

On Christmas day as I walked out
For air and exercise
The hills were bleak and menacing
Grey shrouded were the skies;
But the sight of that lone rose
Brought sunshine to my soul,
Resurrecting all my thoughts
To a poetic goal.

FEBRUARY

F rost encrusted catkins now
E mbroider hazel's pliant bough,
B uds of celandines are swelling,
R aucous rooks nest sites are telling,
U pward thrust daffodil spears,
A pt and authentic pioneers.
R un the streams from icebound places,
Y earn all hearts for springtime graces.

THE BARREN TREE

I viewed with joy the barren tree
That winter's hand had dressed,
'Though quite bereft of fruit or leaf,
Yet it was richly blessed.
At every twiglet's tip there danced
A raindrop, glittering, bright,
Which caught and held the sun's pale beams
And lit with jewelled light
The stark and barren winter's tree
It was a lovely sight to see!

I had viewed with joy this self same tree
Thick creamed with flower in May,
Its beauty haunted the mind's eye
Re-kindling thoughts this day;
Could raindrops vie with springtime blooms?
Or clothe a tree so fair?
Could I deny that this was so,
For loveliness was there.
Upon that stark and barren tree
God's handiwork was plain to see.

ALL CONVINCING

Himalayan mountain peaks,
Polar region's snow,
Sahara's drifting sand,
Amazon's great flow
And a violet sweet and small
God created all.

Antarctica's vast icebergs,
Grand Canyon's awesome scene,
Niagara's roaring torrent,
Rainforests 'lush and green'
And a dewdrop on a leaf
See and own belief.

A gigantic redwood tree,
Wild lions in a pride,
Australia's barrier reef
The moving ocean's tide
And a tiny busy bee
Truly convince me.

ST IVES

Narrow winding streets — flowers in profusion
Cats on harbour walls — asleep
Cats in boats — asleep
Cats beneath upturned boats — asleep.
Painters, capturing the brilliant light,
The quaint cottages — rioting flowers
And cats — asleep and people, awake or asleep.
Sea — blue green, silver grey —
Molten metal, liquid aquamarine,
Foaming, frenzied, fascinating;
Seaweed, shells, sand
And sand patterns, drawn by the tide:
The Tate — and more patterns, drawn by artists,
Fishermen, the lifeboat, the toy town train,
Scenic coastal paths
Winding streets and steps
Cats on steps — asleep.
Art galleries
And beauty
Natural and changing,
Reproduced and permanent
St Ives —
One of England's gems.

A SPRINGTIME GREETING

'Hello lovely primroses,
How good it is again
To see your gentle faces
Fresh washed by springtime rain;
You lend a subtle fragrance,
A telling certainty,
That along your tranquil pathway
Other joys will be.'

A following of bluebells,
Beneath translucent beech,
An overflow of blossoms,
Hawthorn, cherry, peach,
A blush of rambling roses
And later in the year,
A wealth of wild berries,
Autumnal gifts of cheer.

Time passes and so swiftly
Each Christmas comes and goes,
The crocus torches shine,
The firstborn snowdrop blows,
Crinkled leaves and waking blooms
Thrust through departing time.
'Hello lovely primroses,
How sweet 'though brief your time.'

CHAMPAGNE BREAKFAST

Sparrows are having their breakfast
Their tablecloth being our lawn,
They've been chirping in anticipation
Since the early hours of dawn,
Waiting for scraps from our table
To be thrown in the daily routine;
Mothers, fathers and offspring
Gather in their arboured canteen.

Sparrows are drinking their champagne,
From goblets of crimson and blue,
Sipping the nectar sweet liquor,
Distilled from the fresh morning dew,
Deep cupped in the hearts of the flowers;
Fulfilled are their needs — and I smile,
For I know they will be, back again for their tea,
This thought makes a poem worthwhile.

TO FALLEN TREES

Like soldiers on a battlefield, they lie, twisted, broken, slain,
Their conflict with the elements lost — they will not fight again.
Many winters through they faced the foes, of blizzard, gale and flood
And greeted springs victoriously, renewed with fresh life blood
Which surged in every limb and branch, waking buds and fruits to feed;
Rich sap nurtured by England's soil. (How England's heart must bleed!)
As mine does — for these gallant trees, that graced coppice, lane and field;

They fought their fight with power and might; but sadly had to yield,
To storm force winds that flailed and wrenched with strange ferocity,
Like some invading monster on a wild destructive spree —
Intent on vandalism, who pulled trees up roots and all,
Leaving human souls bewildered and bereft to see them fall.
We shall mourn our towering beeches, sweet chestnuts, mighty oak,
The rare and handsome hornbeam, for we are mindful folk;
But the fallen trees will be replaced, in time by those who care,
So that our children's children, may experience, keep and share
The great delight that we have known, in trees beautiful and grand;
Farewell to you our fallen friends — and welcome to our land,
A future generation of saplings straight and young,
In you as in our children — is hope eternal sprung.

IVY LEAVES

Look at the ivy leaves today,
Fluttering in the breeze
In the hedges, over banks,
And garland hung in trees.

Every leaf is different
'Though in species all the same,
Some black-green as winter's yew
Some touched by autumn flame.

Lovely tapestries they weave
Clothing thick and warm,
Cold walls of stone and mortar
Where birds hide safe from harm.

Look at the ivy leaves today,
Bright polished in the sun,
Pick a random posy
And examine every one.

Leaves as small as babies nails
Vein laced in palest green,
Dappled leaves — matt surfaced leaves,
Leaves with cut glass sheen.

Look at the ivy leaves today;
But really look — and see
Beyond the common ivy
The creative intricacy.

THE TIVERTON ASH

Nothing living to be seen
All was concrete, lacking green,
Houses, walls, stone or brick red
No foliage or grass to tread;
Walking down a Tiverton street
No fallen leaves caressed the feet;
Around a corner by a wall,
Standing bravely four feet tall
I spied a solitary tree,
How I longed to set it free,
From tight confine 'twixt stone and gate,
Alas my finding was too late.
Its roots below the pavement went,
Seeded down through minute vent;
About seven years, its age, I guessed,
With this small tree the street was blessed;
Then life refreshing rain came down,
Succouring this Devonshire town
And as I felt it touch my face,
Hope for this ash tree grew apace,
Tenacious roots — sustaining showers
Two more decades — a tree that towers.

LAID TO REST

Gardening was his favourite pastime,
He knew the season and fruition
Of every vegetable, fruit and flower.
Knew when to plant, to feed, to hoe, to harvest:
A wealth of knowledge lay stored
In his aged brain;
But his body would no longer obey his commands;
Frame bent — bones dried, breath shortened
And flesh wearied —
He passed all his beloved tools
To his son-in-law,
Who loaded them on to a trailer
And took them to the nearest rubbish tip,
Grassed his whole garden
And bought all his vegetables and fruit,
From the supermarket.
The old gardener died —
His knowledge died with him
Both laid to rest
Under the churchyard turf.
What a loss to his village,
What a loss to his country
What a loss to England!

EVERGREEN

From the depth of the woodland we gathered,
Berried holly, ivy and pine,
Snow fresh and scented of winter
And a breath of old Christmas time.

Our hearts were so joyful and happy
With this wealth of the wood in our arms,
Evergreen — a sign of the season,
Ever certain to add to its charms.

From the depth of the woodland we hurried,
Swift home to a heart warming scene,
To firelight, mincepies and carols
And Christmas — ever new, evergreen.

THE BREATH OF DEVON

Cool ferny woods — leaf dappled lanes,
Winging geese in ordered skeins,
The gold brocade of whin clothed moor,
Calling gulls on white fringed shore;
Secretive streams — exuberant weirs
Sun speckled trout and shy eyed deer.
Country crafts from days gone by,
Rich soil, green grass and changing sky;
Apple orchards flushed with bloom,
The subtle scent of primrosed coombe,
Bluebells misting wayside banks —
For all of this, we give God thanks,
For this the breath of Devon.

HAPPINESS

Happiness is a sun
Which rises and sets
Within the spirit of man.
Happiness is warmth and light,
It is free and available to all;
But not always easily attained.
Happiness is much sought after,
Many travel far and wide
In search
Of elusive happiness;
Some find all their happiness,
In one spot on earth.
Happiness,
'Though found in the smallest of things
Is indeed the greatest of things.
It is spread throughout the world;
Yet may be held in one tiny hand.
Happiness is finding the good in all people,
It is sharing and enjoying
One another's talents.
Happiness is discovering
One's true self
And working to improve this discovery,
Happiness is making faith and hope
Daily companions.
Happiness is loving and being loved.

SO GREAT AN HERITAGE

Our churches are beautiful
Great monuments to byegone praise
And towers of strength in present days,
Sure hope for all our future ways,
So great an heritage.
By craftsmen skilled their beauty wrought
Where teachers of God's word have taught
And many to repentance brought
The churches of old England.
Here folk have worked, sung hymns and prayed,
Tapestries wove and flowers arrayed,
Wept, laughed and steadfast faith displayed
Within their hallowed walls.
Our churches are beautiful,
May we this generation keep
Them so — as those who round them sleep,
Did likewise toil, that we might reap
So great an heritage.

OLD LYNCH

'Old Lynch' — that lovely spot,
The place where I was born,
Enclosed by apple orchards,
Green meadows — fields of corn,
How full and happy was each day,
Of every changing season,
For every joy a purpose,
For every hour a reason.

Springtime — came the seeking out,
Of nests, shrewdly concealed —
Gatherings of primroses,
From choice nooks in 'Walnut Field';
Summer brought the picnic days,
'Midst rows of hay newmown,
And picking of the soft fruits,
Within our vast garden grown.

Autumn — compelled the tasting,
Of an apple from each tree,
And the shaking down of hazel nuts —
Plus the cider making spree.
Winter was a cosy time,
With crackling logs ablaze,
Holly hunting through the snow,
Tinselled pine on which to gaze.

'Old Lynch' — that lovely house,
Alas no more it stands,
Razed by the bulldozers to dust,
With great metallic hands;
But those joyous childhood days,
Will live with me forever;
'Home of my inspiration,
The root of my endeavour'.

CONVOLVULUS DAWN

Tentative mists
Of approaching Autumn
Rise from earth's hollows
As dawn blinks her eye:
Trumpeters salute the new day,
Riding high upon the crest
Of Buddleia's blue waves,
Weaving through the wattle fence,
Wandering up the willow
Wantonly, to wreath
Her weeping brow.
This twisting, tormenting.
Tenacious weed — loathed by gardeners,
Beautifies the morning,
Heralding the dawn.
White and pure,
Dew jewelled;
In its hour of glory
Convolvulus
Is redeemed.

A NEW YEAR PRAYER

Tread lightly on the threshold,
Young spirit of New Year,
We welcome you with hopeful hearts,
Hearts sore in need of cheer
Tread lightly and tread slowly
Life's pace it seems too fast;
Bring with you a calming influence
And tranquillity to last.

Spread your gifts among us
We need them every one,
Sympathetic tears of rain
Rejoying smiles of sun
Gentle caressing breezes,
To blow troubles far away;
Come enter and illuminate
Each hour of each new day.

Bring us new wealths of wisdom
To preserve our lovely land,
Bring new love for one another,
That we give and not demand,
Bring good into the hearts of men,
Let wars and conflicts cease;
Tread lightly spirit of the year
And scatter seeds of peace.

SOUNDS OF HOPE

Bells — Shatter the iced stillness
Of the winter's night;
Dropping silver sparkles
Of sounds
From towers and steeples
Throughout the land.
Ears receive their age old message;
The child turns in slumber,
Awakened momentarily —
Smiles sleepily — tomorrow?
The mother tending her sick babe
Smiles — perhaps this coming year
He will feel better?
Hope is carried on re-echoing notes
And falls upon celebrating crowds
Outside inns and taverns,
In city squares — in country villages;
Bells — shatter the iced stillness
Of the winter's air,
Ringing out the old year,
Ringing in a brand new morn,
Ears receive — hearts transmit,
Hope is again reborn.

THE BLESSING

Through the greenest green heart
Of Exmoor we drove,
Beneath arboured beeches
And by emerald grove;
We stopped for a picnic
By fern dappled stream
On fresh verdant grass,
Glossed by the sun's beam.

How green was the heartland
Of Exmoor this hour,
With a newness, a freshness
In each nook and bower
And as we looked up,
To the light as it came
Through translucent leafage,
It was like a green flame.

Like a green flame from heaven
Sent directly to bless,
A few modest mortals —
And holiness
Seemed to pervade
The pure woodland air,
A sweet benediction
Was there.

THE AWAKENING

When in the darkest night,
A single thought awakes
And breaks the dream
Into a thousand pieces,
Hinge that thought
Upon a star
To beam afar.

That in the light
A gathering
of thoughts
Combine,
Through poetry
To shine.

In the darkest night
Throughout the globe
Who knows,
What tentacles of wisdom
Seek and probe? —
Human minds
A billion thoughts
To mould and shape,
Literature to perpetuate.

GOOD FRIDAY

Even the lilies cried,
The trees shed tears
And silent meres
Their sympathies supplied.

All lowly creatures there,
Tortoise and snail
Rock dove and quail
Were clothed about with care.

Even the dancing brook
Of joy was stilled;
The whole earth spilled
Its woe, but man forsook.

The corn hung low its head
And grasses bowed,
The wind allowed
A sigh — for love that bled.

For love so strong — that ran
In drops of blood,
A silent flood,
Forgiveness for all man.

THE BUTTERCUP FIELD

The buttercup field was lovely
Thick braided with green at the seams,
Laid like a great golden bedspread,
I picture it now in my dreams;
Out of school and dancing for joy,
Barefoot in flowers and grass,
Shoes in the hand, sun on the face,
Through summers reluctant to pass.

Chained buttercup bracelets we wore
And crowns of bright gold on our hair,
And all the problems of classrooms,
Fell off from our shoulders right there.
Weedkillers and sprays now produced
Both make for good pasture we're told;
But the buttercup field was lovely
And man is fast spending his gold.

HARVEST TRAGEDY

She chose her nest carefully
Well hidden in the corn,
She laid her eggs, olive, smooth
Upon a summer morn,

Settled down, gave of her warmth
To the developing young,
Blissfully unaware
That harvest had begun.

The combine thundered nearer
Still she hugged them tight;
But felt as though her heart would burst,
So loud it beat with fright.

At last the pheasant spread her wings,
Her young she could not save.
Premature their harvest
As cradle became grave.

WHY?

I feel so angry when I see
A plastic bag up a tree,
Or empty cans carelessly thrown
Where wild primroses have sown
Tiny seedings sweet and young,
Or view a briar rose bestrung
With tattered paper old and soiled,
Why is this beauty so despoiled?
I feel so saddened when I look
At crisp bags strewn by fern fringed brook.

Have those who scatter rubbish o'er,
Woodland, wayside, beach and moor,
No thought or love for Nature's worth
That they so degrade this earth?
I feel so angry and defeated
To see our lovely land so treated!
Campaigns are started every year
To keep our lanes and byways clear;
Somehow they never quite succeed
In this age of packaged greed.
Why? when most folk are neat and clean
Is there so much rubbish to be seen
And I ask what can be done?
To instil in everyone
A sense of patriotic pride
Suffice to cleanse our countryside.

A VILLAGE MOURNS

Heads bowed and clothed in sadness
In little groups they came,
Eyes drawn to one small coffin
In every heart one name,
Shaun — their playmate and their friend
Why why this tragic, sudden end?

Sunlight through the stained glass panes
Fell on each wet young face,
Springtime flowers in the porch
Lay massed in every space;
Strains of Largo filled the air
And all those who loved Shaun were there.

And every mother's heart ached
And felt Her sorrow too;
And every caring father,
Could feel His pain right through;
And all the village mourned as one
The loss of a beloved son.

Thorverton was united
In grief for this young boy
Who loved life and lent to it
His special kind of joy;
And 'though his earthly life is gone,
In loving hearts he will live on.

THE FOUR SEASONS

When daffodils nod golden heads,
And violets peep from leafy beds,
When birds are busy in the trees,
And earth's swept clean by the gentle breeze;
When in woods green buds are breaking,
And all around new life is waking,
To God a prayer of thanks we bring,
For this lovely gift of SPRING.

When roses bloom in gardens fair,
And honeysuckle scents the air,
When butterflies fan brilliant wing,
And fledglings learn to soar and sing;
When pollen laden bees buzz nigh,
And sea reflects the azure sky;
To God give thanks in song and rhyme,
For giving us sweet SUMMER time.

When apples in the orchards blush,
And on the rowan feeds the thrush,
When ripened rosehips flame the briar,
And trees together do conspire,
To beautify in gold and red,
And 'Harvest Home' secures our bread,
To God we lift our voice in praise,
For these mellow AUTUMN days.

When frost suspends with icy hand,
And flowers sleep throughout the land,
When boughs and twigs are crystal cased,
And weeds and fronds bejewelled and laced;
When pristine snow cloaks starlit view,
And all the world looks bright and new,
To God we 'carol' loud and clear.
For WINTER'S balm and Christmas cheer.

A CAT POEM (TO WEASEL)

'Feed the cat,' that's what I say:
Morning and evening
And middle of day;
Does she deserve it
All this service to her?
On occasions she deigns
To give me a purr;
But she is lazy and sleepy
Most of the day
And never, but never
Has that much to say.
She doesn't catch mice (thinks hunting absurd)
And just winks an eye at an impudent bird,
Lies on my prize blooms,
Digs pits in the border
And when a kitten, caused much disorder;
Now she has reached
The ripe age of ten,
A milestone, which made me reach for a pen
And write this short ditty
To 'WEASEL' — my cat,
Who with love in her eyes
Close by me is sat
And how I shall miss her
When she leaves me forever
For a cat's companion
Who finds fault with one never.

A CAT POEM (TO THOMAS)

High upon the rooftop tiles
Like a wise old owl he's sat
With wide and ever watchful eyes,
Our next door neighbour's cat.
He wears a proud and haughty look,
Of his cat land he is king
His eyes, his claws and wits are sharp
And he fears not anything.

And when he deigns to spring to ground
His territory to roam,
All other felines hereabout
Beat quick retreats to home:
And all the dogs that nearby dwell
Of him are rather shy
And with their tails between their legs
With haste indoors do fly.

The saying goes, that each cat has
Nine lives; but he
Has used them up and I feel sure
Earned immortality.
A vital character this puss
With mysterious air of fame
At best or worse inspiring verse
'Thomas Dylan' is his name.

THE AUTUMN LEAF

Fluttering like a butterfly
I chanced to see it fall
And held out my hand instinctively
Its downward drift to stall;
And there it lay upon my palm
A symbol of the season —
Why the desire to take it home?
I knew no logic reason:
Except that it was attractive,
Held the sunlight of the year
And a certain whispered promise
That new leaves would soon appear;
Fragile as silk unfurled in spring,
It had weathered many a storm
And withstood pests and pestilence
Keeping purity of form.
One unique, perfect leaf of gold
I pressed, then framed and cherished
What kindly breeze brought it to me?
While all its kin lie perished.

AN EXPLORATION

A poppy seedhead, wrinkled, dried
lay upon the floor
On retrieving it, I found
It led me to explore
The mystery and wonder
Of birth and death — and life;
A minute case of blackened seed
Burst open — thoughts were rife.
I held a seed within my hand,
Small and hard; but dead?
No! — before my eyes there blew
A drift of poppies red,
Scarlet satin petals waved,
A vision given me
While in my hand there lay
Hope of eternity.

INSPIRATION

I ridescent colours from fountains shine
N uminous dawn crowns mountain tops divine,
S ongbirds spill silver notes — this arboured choir
P erchance a poet somewhere may inspire.
I lluminations of moon, stars and sun,
R adiate and animate earth's confine;
A eolian music floats to be re-spun
T hrough trees and ferns, through reeds and briar;
I ntricate patterns print the land's attire.
O ceans, seas, symphonically combine
N ature's inspirations transfuse design.

TO LIFE A LIGHT

Poetry is the perceptive power
To draw forth beauty from a flower
And show it to unseeing eyes,
In new and e'en more lovely guise.
Poetry is to life a light
Penetrating darkest night,
Illuminating mind and thought,
In its beams are maxims caught
And held in print — passed down through ages,
Spilt from the souls of long dead sages.
Poetry is a binding chain —
Addictive as a fine champagne;
Poetry is beyond this earth,
Beyond out time, beyond our birth,
It reaches out from somewhere vast.
We are primed, engulfed, surpassed;
Poetry holds the poet in its control,
Wills him to write, read and extol.
To him it is fulfilment's breath
To lose the gift — a kind of death.

BLOSSOMS

Frothy, foamy, white capped waves,
Land fostered — far from seas
Lap and break and overspill
O'er country lanes and leas;
Like billowed sails — like drifted snow,
Clouds fleeced in purest white,
Cherry, sloe and hawthorn vie
To fill us with delight;
Blossoms breathing loveliness
Crowding springtime days,
If you would capture beauty's heart
Pick one small bloom and gaze,
For all that beauty is contained
Within a single flower;
And nothing man has ever made
To gladden has such power.

THE CHAIN OF LIFE

When the celandines are over
The buttercups will shine,
As their gold begins to tarnish
Blooms the wild woodbine,
As these climbers drop their petals,
Fruit and firethorn will glow;
So the chain of life continues
Through falling leaves, to falling snow.

When the blanket of the winter
Recedes and earth awakes,
Springtime still surprises mortals
As each sleepy soul she shakes,
Once again tired eyes are opened
To the glory of the world,
And all the wonders of creation
Successively unfurled.

BELIEF

It seems to me I have believed
From the time I was conceived,
For there's no memory in my heart
Of when belief was not a part
Of all that I am or have been;
Belief is as the grass is green,
A thrusting, growing, springing sign
Of life in all its great design.
It seems to me a minute seed
From mighty tree or lowly weed,
Does capsulate mankind's belief,
To bring it forth in every leaf;
For however could such wonders be
If no creator held the key?
I ask not from whence do these thoughts rise,
'Dawn is the light in morning skies'.

POETRY IS ENGLAND

Poetry is England
With all its many faces
Its glory and its grandeur
Its gentleness and graces:
Poetry is England,
This dear beloved isle
Has birthed some of the greatest,
Who've made living here worthwhile;
They have left us with a wondrous wealth
Of literature supreme:
Poetry is England —
England a poet's dream.

THE LAST STRAW

The old bridge
Had stood for many generations:
Horses and carts,
Barrows and bicycles,
Cattle and cars,
The old bridge
Had seen them all
And withstood
Time, tempest and torrent;

The articulated lorry
Was the last straw,
— that broke the bridges back;
But the river flowed on —
Memories of the old bridge
Were written
In its music
And would flow
Through time.

THIS IS MY LAND

This is my land, wherein my days are spent
I am so grateful I have a while been lent
This island green and fair, that I call my own
And all its dear and lovely ways,
Delightfully familiar and well known.

This is my land, these gentle fields enclosed
By hedges swathed in green, trees beautifully posed
And curving waterways, where streamlets merge in song
With river's unremitting flow,
As one to reach the sea, where all belong.

Thus is my land, wherein my roots lie deep
Here dwell my kith and kin, here my ancestors sleep
To England I am bound, by love's most precious chain
I would not break these life long bonds
For greater, richer lands or worldly gain.